TRENCH WARFARE.

NOTES ON ATTACK AND DEFENCE.

COLLATED BY THE GENERAL STAFF.

February, 1915.

The Naval & Military Press Ltd

Published by

The Naval & Military Press Ltd
Unit 5 Riverside, Brambleside
Bellbrook Industrial Estate
Uckfield, East Sussex
TN22 1QQ England

Tel: +44 (0)1825 749494

www.naval-military-press.com
www.nmarchive.com

In reprinting in facsimile from the original, any imperfections are inevitably reproduced and the quality may fall short of modern type and cartographic standards.

PREFACE.

The notes herein contained mainly consist of, or are drawn from, memoranda which have been published for the information and guidance of the troops at the front. They prescribe no hard and fast methods for attack or defence, and they deal exclusively with the conduct of those operations as limited by the conditions under which the fighting has assumed much of the character of siege warfare. This phase may not endure ; but, in any case, so far as general principles are concerned, the doctrine expounded in Field Service Regulations holds good.

Among the salient points which are brought out are the necessity for systematic preparation, down to the smallest detail, before the delivery of an attack ; the vital importance of the most intimate co-operation between artillery and infantry ; the fact that, since the capture of trenches is generally easier than their retention, means whereby the difficulty of the latter may be overcome require the most careful preparation and consideration in advance ; and, finally, the necessity for counter-attacking without a moment's delay, whether in defence against the enemy's attacking troops, or against his counterstroke after an attack has been successfully delivered.

TRENCH WARFARE.

NOTES ON ATTACK AND DEFENCE.

I.—AN EXAMPLE OF INSTRUCTIONS ISSUED REGARDING LOCAL ATTACKS WHEN THE OPPOSING FORCES ARE AT CLOSE QUARTERS.

The general considerations which should guide a commander in organizing and preparing a local attack against a strongly entrenched enemy have been pointed out in previous memoranda. The present instructions aim at laying down in detail the steps to be taken in the carrying out of such an attack, with special reference to the infantry.

It appears, from reports recently received, that many of the assaults made by the infantry on the enemy's trenches are launched and developed on lines similar to those of an ordinary attack. A few scouts advance first and reach the line of the enemy's wire entanglements, where they are very soon put out of action in full view of the leading detachments waiting in the trenches. This does not tend to heighten the moral of these detachments. They leave their trenches with reluctance, move forward slowly, and often return more quickly. Sometimes they suffer considerable loss in passing through their own barbed wire, through which perhaps only one passage has been made. The attack fails and is not renewed.

This is not the way to prepare and to carry out at close quarters an operation which is rather in the nature of an assault than of an ordinary attack.

It is essential that the most minute details should be thought out and prepared, in order that the detachments detailed for the assault may all leave their trenches at the same moment and reach the objective at one rush without firing a shot.

The steps to be taken are as follows:—

(1.) A definitely limited objective must be selected.
(2.) The objective and the enemy's means of defence, including the flank defence of the trenches forming the objective, must be thoroughly reconnoitred (aeroplanes).
(3.) Troops for the assault, and other troops for covering the flanks of the assault by fire, must be detailed.
(4.) The assaulting troops must be assembled opposite their objective in several columns, each column including a detachment of engineers provided with explosives for destroying the defences.

(5.) Supports for each assaulting column, and reserves, must be detailed and organized.
(6.) A different route must be allotted to each column.
(7.) Means whereby trenches can be crossed (ladders or gangways) must be provided, so that all the columns may debouch rapidly and simultaneously.
(8.) The barbed wire entanglements must be arranged so that there may be as many passages through it as there are assaulting columns.

At a given signal the artillery must lengthen its range, so as to build up a wall of fire behind the enemy's first line, while batteries posted on the flanks continue to bombard the objective with high explosive shell.

On this signal being given the assault must be launched in one rush; this is essential if it is to succeed.

The energy and courage of the troops will do the rest.

Lastly the special attention of officers commanding is drawn to the absolute necessity for entrusting the carrying out of the attack to reserve troops* coming from behind the line of trenches. There is no doubt that troops occupying the first line trenches have an instinctive reluctance to quitting their accustomed cover. These troops should be used to afford flanking protection to the attacking troops, to support them by covering fire, and to constitute a body upon which they can fall back if eventually it should be found necessary to do so.

II.—A LOCAL ATTACK.

(*See* Plate 1.)

EXAMPLE OF ORDERS FOR THE ATTACK.

The attack, the orders for which follow, was carried out by part of the troops of a division which held over three miles of front. No additional troops were sent up to reinforce the division in anticipation of or during the attack. Of the 12 battalions available, six were detailed for the attack (including the two battalions in reserve). Four battalions held the trenches in the vicinity of the points attacked. Two battalions were left to hold the remaining 1½ miles of the line.

The artillery bombardment began at 9 a.m. By 9.45 a.m. the obstacles were sufficiently broken up to provide a lane for each assaulting column through the wire entanglement. The artillery

---

* The troops detailed to carry out the assault must previously be given ample opportunity to accustom themselves to their surroundings in the actual positions from which the attack is to be launched, and to become familiar with the various features in the objective assigned to them.

was ordered to lengthen the range, the assault was made at the same time, and the trenches were captured with about 60 of the enemy in them.

The enemy then opened a bombardment with heavy artillery, which was very severe for about an hour. The troops in D trench were eventually forced to give ground, but re-occupied the trench after being reinforced from the reserve.

The enemy made no infantry counter-attack on this day, and by the following evening the remaining trenches of the group referred to in the Orders for the Attack had been taken, and machine guns had been pushed down into the ravine running north-east of hill 180.

The attackers' losses on the first day amounted to about 500 in all, and were almost entirely caused by artillery fire.

ORDERS FOR THE ATTACK.

1. An attack will be made on the enemy's positions north of B . . .
2. *Objective.*—The objective will be the enemy's trenches marked D, B, E, M, on Plate L, facing our trenches 5, 6, 7, 8, 9.
3. *Attacking troops.*—The troops detailed for the attack are :—

  6 infantry battalions.
  2 companies engineers.*

4. *Distribution.*—The attacking troops will be formed in two columns (which will attack side by side) and a reserve as follows :—

Left column.	*Right column.*
2 infantry battalions.	2 infantry battalions.
½ company engineers.	½ company engineers.

Reserve.
2 Infantry battalions.*

5. *Direction of attack.*—The left column will cross trenches 5, 6 and 7 by gangways; it will seize trenches D and E, drive out the defenders and occupy the communication trenches sufficiently far forward for purposes of protection. A detachment previously detailed for the purpose will face west; another similarly detailed will face east, and will enfilade trench B with a machine gun.

As soon as the left column has reached the hostile trenches, the right column will debouch by trenches 8 and 9, and advance through the interval between them against trenches M and W. Successive colums will be sent up at once to reinforce, and every effort will be made to advance eastward.

At the same time the left column will attack trench B.

If the attack succeeds, the attacking force will endeavour to push on to the east by trenches S, T, V, Y, Z; it will thus be possible to take trenches R and Q in front and flank, and perhaps to capture them.

---

* In the copy of orders received, further mention of the second engineer company is omitted. Presumably it was allotted to the reserve.

As soon as the engineers with the attacking columns are in the enemy's trenches, they will search for mines and cut the fuzes.

As each trench is successively captured, the infantry will begin to place it in a state of defence with the utmost rapidity. With this in view, all communication trenches leading to the captured trench will be held by small bodies of picked men about 50 paces from the point of junction, thus forming a covering party behind which all other available men can work at the conversion of the main trench. Materials found on the spot will be used, and coils of barbed wire, sandbags, *chevaux-de-frise*, &c., will be collected beforehand in the communication trenches of 6, 7, 8 and 9.

6. *Machine guns.*—The machine guns of the left column, which will have been engaged in destroying the wire entanglements, will follow the supports of the attacking columns, and will take up a position in trench E to hold the front. One machine gun will enfilade trench B. The machine gun sections of the right column will also follow the supports, and will occupy trenches M and S, so as to fire on B, R and Q.

7. *Flank protection for the attack.*—In addition to the flanking detachments ordered to face outwards as soon as the trenches are reached, the infantry attacks will be covered as follows:—

(*a.*) By fire from trenches 1, 2, 3 and 4 (rifle and machine gun).

(*b.*) By fire from trench 9, so long as this is not masked by the attacking columns, and from the trenches on hill 180.

(*c.*) By the naval and mountain guns on hills 180 and 165, and by the field batteries.

8. *Organization of the attacking columns.*—The assault will be made in each battalion by three companies simultaneously. Each company will be in four columns—one platoon to each column.* Each platoon will have one section leading, followed by a party of engineers, then a second section; the third and fourth sections, similarly organized with a party of engineers between them, will follow almost immediately. Every column will be given two light wooden gangways for crossing each of our own trenches.

Men will carry their entrenching tools in their belts. Every third man will carry a pick or shovel drawn from the tool carts, or from the engineers. Every man will carry a sandbag. Six men of the leading section will carry a hurdle for getting over wire entanglements. The leading six men of each column will be given wire-cutters. All men except those of the leading section of each column will wear their packs.

9. *Assembly of columns before the assault.*—Companies will be drawn up before the assault in the communication trenches, and at places of assembly near the first line trenches. Assaulting columns will be organized beforehand as shown.

---

* Line of platoons in fours or file is probably meant.

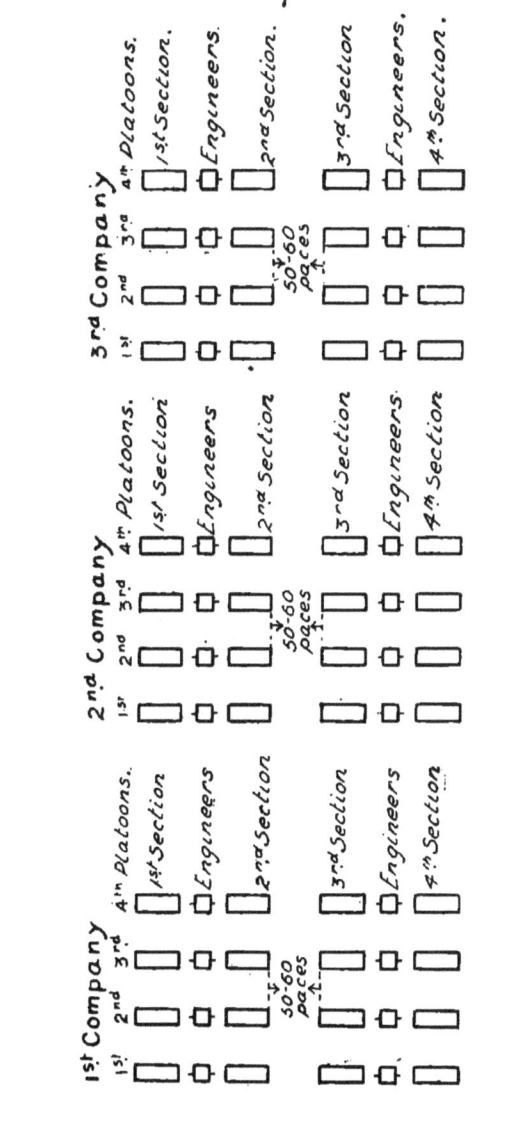

Special instructions have been issued regarding the place of assembly of each battalion.

10. *Preparation of the attack.*—The preparation of the attack will be made as follows :—

(a.) Generally speaking, the field artillery will engage any hostile battery that opens fire. Certain batteries have been detailed for the destruction of the wire entanglements by their fire, and for the demolition of the enemy's trenches.

(b.) The naval and mountain guns will engage the enemy's machine guns. The trench-mortars will bombard the enemy's trenches.

(c.) The fortress machine guns will, by their fire, make breaches in the entanglements wherever the latter are visible.

When the required effect has been produced by the above means the artillery will lengthen its range. At a signal prearranged between the officer commanding and the C.R.A. the infantry will rush forward, led by its officers and non-commissioned officers.

11. *The assault.*—If the assault is to succeed it must be carried out with all the rapidity and energy of which officers and men are capable. The secondary defences must be dest·oyed and crossed, the trenches must be carried, the defenders killed, and a defence rapidly formed to meet a counter-attack, whether delivered immediately or after an interval of delay.

12. *The reserve.*—The reserve battalions will be in the ravine west of hill 180 during the attack. When the attack has begun one battalion will be held in readiness to move by the communication trenches, or in extended formation, to the places of assembly near trenches 6 to 8. The other battalion will remain under cover.

13. Should the attacking columns be forced to retire, in which case heavier losses will be incurred than if they hold their ground, they will fall back on the troops occupying the trenches.

14. *Engineer stores.*—The engineer stores will be placed close to the entrance to the communication trenches, and near trenches 6 and 8.

15. *Ammunition.*—There will be carried on the man 200 rounds, and a reserve of 300,000 rounds will be formed behind the trenches in the ravine west of hill 180.

Trench-mortars will have several reserve supplies placed at different points in the deep casemates.

16. *Troops in the trenches.*—The rôle of the troops in the trenches will be as follows :—

(a.) To cover the flank of the attack. This applies especially to the troops holding trenches 1, 2, 3 and 4. Those holding trenches 10 to 20 will cover the ground to their front so long as their fire is not masked by the attack.

(b.) Troops holding trenches 20 to 26 will engage any bodies trying to debouch from the valley north-east of hill 180, or from the ravines to the north, and will also maintain a heavy fire on the enemy's trenches in order to force his troops to remain under cover.

Detailed orders will be given to trench commanders in order to ensure the distribution of fire from the moment that the attack begins over those of the enemy's trenches which are not attacked. In trenches 25 and 26 special observers will be stationed; they will watch the progress of the attack carefully and see that our fire against the enemy's trenches does not hamper it.

III.—MEMORANDUM ON METHODS OF ATTACK WHICH HAVE PROVED SATISFACTORY.

Essential factors.—The essential factors may shortly be tabulated as follows:—

(a.) The objective must be chosen with a view to artillery co-operation in the preparation of the attack, and to the concentration of artillery fire thereupon.
(b.) The fullest possible information with regard to that part of the enemy's position which it is decided to attack must be obtained by means of reconnaissance.
(c.) Arrangements must be made for a suitable distribution of artillery fire over the various defences, batteries, trenches, &c., of the enemy.
(d.) Arrangements must be made for protecting the infantry by artillery fire against counter-attack after the position has been taken, and until such time as the ground gained has been made good.
(e.) The artillery should range repeatedly on the several targets allotted to it, until by careful observation of the results it is clearly established that the required effect can be produced.
(f.) The action of the artillery and infantry must be simultaneous and combined.
(g.) In order to make good the ground gained, the fullest co-operation between engineers and infantry is necessary.

1. *Preliminary.*—The present phase of the operations approximates to siege warfare; and methods of attack which are not based on realization of this fact have proved not only costly but unsuccessful.

2. *Objective.*—The extent of the actual objective of each attack must be limited by the necessity for ensuring a sufficient concentration of artillery fire upon it. Such an objective may be a line of trenches not more than 500 yards in extent. But other

portions of the enemy's line should be attacked and bombarded at the same time, in order to keep the defenders occupied and to distract their attention from the true objective.

3. *Front.*—The front should be divided into two sections, an offensive section and a defensive section. The latter should be lightly held, and the operations undertaken in this part of the line (local attacks, saps, bombardments) should be calculated to draw the enemy's attention from the remainder of the front. The section of the front on which the attack is to be driven home should be selected with a view to securing the most favourable conditions for the co-operation of the artillery, and its extent must depend upon the amount of artillery which can be concentrated in that part of the line.

4. *Reconnaissance.*—Reconnaissances should be carried out by day and by night in order to obtain as detailed information as possible with regard to the enemy's defences, wire entanglements, firing and communication trenches, natural obstacles, the lie of the land, distances, enemy's batteries, &c. All information so gained must be marked on a map for the use of the C.R.A. in the preparation of his arrangements, and these form the basis of the plan of attack.

5. *Rôle of the artillery.*—The rôle of the artillery is fourfold :—

(a.) The engagement and silencing of the enemy's batteries.
(b.) The destruction of the enemy's defences.
(c.) The support of the infantry attack.
(d.) The protection of the infantry against counter-attack.

In order to prevent counter-attacks, it has been found effective to increase the range of the lighter guns so as to establish a wall of fire beyond the line of captured trenches, while the heavier guns continue to engage the enemy's batteries.

6. *Rehearsal of the attack.*—After all the ranges have been ascertained, the artillery should rehearse the part it is to play on several consecutive days, without, however, arousing the suspicion of the enemy by prolonged or intense bombardment. On these occasions the infantry detailed for the attack should be assembled in the positions from which it will have to start when the actual attack is made.

7. *Final preparation.*—On the day of the attack, a final rehearsal should take place, in order to eliminate any errors which might otherwise arise owing to weather conditions, &c.

8. *Orders for the attack.*—Final orders for the infantry attack should not be given until the artillery reports everything in readiness. As a general rule, the attack cannot be delivered on a pre-arranged day and hour, but must depend upon the completion of the artillery preparations. The time required for the infantry to reach their positions of readiness having been ascertained beforehand, and the duration of the bombardment having been decided on, the hour of the attack can be fixed.

9. *Infantry attack.*—(*a.*) The troops in the trenches should not take part in the assault.

(*b.*) The assaulting columns should be massed, under cover, near or in the communication trenches.

(*c.*) The strength of the force detailed for the assault must be determined by the importance of the objective. As a general rule, on fronts of 500 to 800 yards, five battalions and two engineer companies have been found sufficient to carry out the assault and to provide sufficient reinforcements and reserves.

10. *Co-operation between artillery and infantry.*—The essential factor is co-operation between the action of the artillery and the infantry attack. With this end in view repeated rehearsals should take place, and all observing stations should contain an infantry as well as an artillery officer, both being separately connected with their report centres by telephone.

11. *The assault.*—When the C.R.A. reports that all is prepared, final orders should be sent to the infantry to move up to their positions of readiness. The destruction of the enemy's defences should be completed by the concentration of fire on a small area, and the assault should then be launched. As soon as the infantry approaches the enemy's trenches, the artillery must increase its range so as to establish the wall of fire, previously alluded to, behind the enemy's position.

During the whole time that the attack is in progress the troops in the trenches on either flank of the assaulting parties must maintain an incessant fire with rifles and machine guns on the enemy's trenches to the right and left of the position attacked.

IV.—DESCRIPTION OF A SUCCESSFUL ATTACK.

(*See* Plate II.)

The opposing lines were about 300 to 400 yards apart, approximately as shown on Plate II. Along the whole front there was a wire entanglement which would have prevented the troops from moving forward to the attack. A line of trenches was therefore dug in front of the entanglement. These trenches were not deep enough to prevent the infantry from getting out of them very quickly.

A large force of artillery, including some heavy batteries (about 150 guns in all) was brought up to support the attack. Artillery observers were posted in the trenches. Orders were issued for the bombardment of the trenches forming the objective to be carried out as follows:—

    20 minutes heavy bombardment.
    10 minutes interval.
    20 minutes heavy bombardment.
    4 minutes intensive bombardment (by field guns only).

The bombardment, and, in fact, all the arrangements, were worked by the clock, watches being carefully set beforehand.

The interval of 10 minutes was ordered with a view to leading the enemy to believe that the bombardment was over, and in the hope that his troops would leave their bomb-proofs and support trenches and move up into the fire trenches to meet the expected infantry assault.

Towards the end of the second bombardment the infantry detailed for the attack moved out of the front trench and lay ready to advance.

At the exact moment fixed for the intensive bombardment the infantry rose and advanced, and, under cover of the artillery fire, pushed up as close to the enemy's trenches as possible and lay down. Some of the shells of the supporting artillery were falling short of the enemy's trenches, and where this occurred the advancing infantry halted somewhat further back.

The four minutes intensive bombardment stopped at the given moment, and the infantry, after a short pause, rushed to the assault. Some of the heavier guns continued to fire at objectives further to the rear and at certain other targets on the flank (trenches, machine guns and artillery positions).

The infantry rushed the front trenches and found them practically empty, as the enemy during the artillery bombardment had retired into support trenches and bomb-proofs.

Up to this moment the casualties had been slight. The front line of trenches were all captured except a small section on the right of the enemy's line.

The support trenches and bomb-proofs were quite close up to the front line, and communication trenches led into the firing trenches.

As soon as the bombardment ceased and the trenches had been captured, the enemy began to appear, and within a very few minutes had opened a heavy rifle fire on the occupants of the captured trenches. The latter found it very difficult to reply on account of having to use the back of the trenches.

Attempts were made to advance up the communication trenches, but in most cases the enemy checked this by placing a machine gun at the far end.

The enemy then began to attack with bombs, in some cases throwing them from the support trenches, in others working up the communication trenches. The enemy seemed to have an unlimited supply of bombs, and the losses caused by them began to be serious. Reinforcements were sent up, but lost very heavily in crossing the space between the trenches. Two long communication trenches were therefore dug, taking about four hours to complete (AA on Plate II.).

In the meantime the enemy had succeeded in clearing the captured trenches with their bombs, though the attacking troops only fell back a short distance and dug themselves in about 40 or 50 yards away. It is not clear how they were able thus to entrench themselves in the open. Presumably the enemy's guns were unable to fire since the opposing troops were too close together; and while the new trench was out of range of bombs, its occupants were probably able with their own rifle fire to keep down that of the enemy in the trenches.

The fighting ended in the attackers establishing themselves firmly on the line which they had dug just in front of the enemy's trenches (BB on Plate II.). The enemy continued to hold his original line.

There are some important lessons to be learned from these and other operations in which our troops have been engaged.

(i.) A carefully thought out plan is essential. Everything must be prepared down to the most minute particular. Small details are often the most important—in fact, no detail is too small to merit attention.

In the instance described above, the timing of the bombardments and the advance of the attacking infantry worked without a hitch.

(ii.) The effect of properly directed artillery fire is very great. The artillery observers must be up in the front trenches, and between them and the guns there must be quick (telephonic) communication.

(iii.) Some of the guns, at any rate, should be brought up to close range. This enables the gunners to keep their own infantry under close observation, and the guns to be turned quickly on to counter-attacking troops or any fresh target.

(iv.) The capture of the enemy's trenches often presents little difficulty. The problem usually is how to keep them. This requires much previous consideration and preparation, and nothing should be left to chance. After capturing a line of trenches, efforts should immediately be made to work outwards, so as to counter the enemy's attempts to retake it. The counter-attack is very frequently made by working laterally from traverse to traverse, and driving out the occupants of the captured trenches by means of bombs and grenades. The enemy's trench-mortars assist in this operation, and have been found very difficult to locate.

(v.) The enemy's wire entanglements usually present considerable difficulty. If they are blown up—except immediately before the attack—the enemy may thereby be put on the alert. Machine guns have sometimes been successfully used to demolish obstacles of this nature.

(vi) The attacking troops were driven out of the captured trenches by bombs. This happens very frequently. It is essential that the attackers themselves should have a plentiful supply of bombs and grenades, and there must be an organized plan for keeping the occupants of a captured trench amply supplied with these missiles in order to meet a counter-attack. The fullest preparations must be made for dealing with the communication or other trenches from which the enemy can throw bombs into the captured trench. If such trenches are straight, machine guns may be posted to enfilade them ; but everything depends on whether the attackers or the defenders are the first to establish their machine guns. If they are zig-zag trenches, men should be pushed down to block them (probably with sandbags) far enough forward to keep the enemy beyond bombing distance.

(vii.) The enemy should be attacked without a moment's hesitation, either by fire or with the bayonet, as soon as he emerges from his support trenches and bomb-proofs.

(viii.) Every detail must be prepared with regard to the support of the troops in the captured trenches, by artillery (single guns pushed close up can do much to help), by concentrated machine gun and rifle fire, and by every other possible means.

(ix.) It will often be advisable to begin digging a communication trench as soon as the enemy's trench is captured.

(x.) Every officer and every man should know exactly what he is to do. This is most important.

The defence requires equal consideration. Arrangements must be made not only to prevent the enemy from capturing trenches but also to drive him out if he should effect a lodgment.

Preparations must be made, and all must be in constant readiness, for an immediate counter-attack with bombs.

All troops must understand what they are to do if the enemy bombards the front trenches heavily. The bomb-proofs and support trenches must be connected with the firing trench. The possibility, in the event of the enemy making a lodgment, of enfilading the captured trench with machine guns or artillery, or both, must be fully considered.

It is unlikely that the enemy will be able to carry out a successful surprise attack. Generally speaking, he will be bound to give indications of his intention, either by a bombardment, or by massing infantry in his saps, or by the close approach of his saps. A careful officer will seldom be surprised, and he will usually be well advised to move his reserves as close as possible to the threatened point.

If the enemy makes a lodgment or pushes on beyond the front line, he should be counter-attacked at once. There is no time to be lost.

V.—MEMORANDUM ON THE ORGANIZATION OF DEFENCE.

It is necessary to prepare the first line of defence in such a way as to make it as nearly as possible unbreakable. The following measures, which have already been carried out on certain portions of the front, are communicated by way of suggestion :—

1. Whenever the situation permits, it is advisable to substitute for continuous trenches a system of centres of resistance or *points d'appui*, either natural or constructed, separated by spaces which must be well flanked and rendered absolutely impassable by obstacles. The nature of those *points d'appui* will vary with the circumstances; it will often be advantageous, particularly in wooded country or on ground little exposed to the enemy's artillery, to make closed works. Whenever it is necessary to retain existing trenches, endeavours should be made to break up the regularity of the front, in order to obtain flanking positions from which the intervening space may be swept by heavy fire. In this way not only will economy of strength be assured, but also strong flanking positions for the fire of infantry, machine guns, and, if necessary, artillery. Daily experience has proved beyond all question the desirability of such a course. Special care should be taken to post machine guns in such a way that they are not only protected and hidden, but also able to fire in several directions.

The *points d'appui* should be protected by strong auxiliary defences, which should surround them almost completely. The wire defences should consist of two entanglements 10 or 12 yards broad, with a distance of 10 or 20 yards between them, the second being hidden from the enemy's sight as far as possible.

As many obstacles as possible should be arranged between the *points d'appui* so as to make the intervals impassable. These intervals should be watched with the greatest care, particularly at night. For this purpose listening posts, themselves protected by wire, and communicating by trenches with the principal defence, may be posted in front of the wire entanglement.

Care must always be taken to leave convenient exits for reconnaissance and attack, by arranging openings protected by easily movable obstacles, and commanded by the covering trenches.

2. As a general principle, troops responsible for the defence of a position should have a shelter behind them to afford protection against shell fire and the weather. This shelter would be reached by a well protected communication trench.

3. At a short distance (100—200 yards) in rear there should be support trenches, made in sections and not continuous, designed to limit the retirement of a party momentarily compelled to evacuate the first line trenches, and to give time for local reserves to come up and counter-attack.

4. A first line, continuous and thinly held throughout, does not allow of the assembly with ease and rapidity of a force strong enough for an attack or a counter-attack. Narrow communication trenches add a further difficulty. In order to obviate these difficulties, *places d'armes* should be made behind, but near the first line. They should consist of trenches large enough to hold at least a company, and may advantageously be subdivided into platoon trenches, connected by communication trenches. They must be easy of access; steps are required if the trench is open, a slope if it is covered.

5. Close co-operation between infantry and artillery is an essential factor of defensive organization. Every effort should be made to improve the means of co-operation. Endeavours should be made to concentrate upon a single zone the fire of as much artillery as possible. Batteries of guns of all calibres should be placed close to the front line, the strength of which will assure their security; they will then be enabled to cope decisively with the German artillery, even at long range. These guns should be protected by epaulments, preferably with overhead cover. Dugouts should be provided, and, where necessary, trenches communicating with the observation posts. These posts themselves should be well protected.

6. The preparation of the second line (not to be confused with the covering trenches) must not be neglected. In many places wire entanglements have not been sufficiently strongly made; they should always be constructed as recommended above for first line entanglements. Shelters should also be provided.

In every section artillery officers should study battery positions suitable for the defence of the second line.

7. These various improvements should be undertaken as early as possible, and carried out with the greatest energy. Apart from their proper use, they will have the further advantage of keeping the men occupied and interested, and of maintaining their physical and moral condition.

VI.—NOTES ON RECENT GERMAN METHODS OF ATTACK.

There are several points in connection with recent attacks from which useful lessons may be derived for future guidance.

ATTACK ON Z

1. This attack was preceded by no artillery preparation. The Germans, in strength about a battalion, emerged from their trenches in daylight, about 8 a.m., and advanced in close formation against the trenches opposite to them, which were well protected

by wire, and were between 200 and 300 yards distant. The enemy appeared to have a second battalion in support and a third in reserve.

2. The defenders were on the look-out and well prepared. The attack was met with rapid and sustained fire under which the enemy suffered heavy losses. Some of the Germans reached the wire entanglement, but none of them succeeded in crossing it.

3. The artillery of the defence kept the enemy's supports and reserves under a continuous bombardment, and, in consequence, no attempt was made to reinforce the battalion which had been launched to the attack.

4. The lessons to be learned from the defeat of this attack are :—

First, the necessity of being constantly on the watch and of being able to bring an overwhelming volume of fire to bear on the enemy at very short notice. The careful selection of machine gun positions will enable commanding officers to reduce the number of men kept in the fire trench. This number should also vary with the state of the ground in front of our trenches, *i.e.*, whether it is deep and heavy, or hard and in a state admitting of a rapid advance being made.

Secondly, the need of having a sufficient force of artillery in close support of the infantry line and ready at short notice to open rapid bursts of fire on any part of the ground between the two lines of trenches or in rear of them where the enemy's supports and reserves are likely to assemble.

ATTACK ON G

5. In this part of the front the two lines of trenches were sc close together that efficient wire entanglements had not been constructed. The attack was preceded by a heavy artillery bombardment lasting more than an hour, and the infantry assault was delivered by four or five companies with great dash and vigour. Several assaults were repulsed, but finally the Germans succeeded in gaining an entrance into the village, through which they advanced until they were checked by the keep or reduit which had been thoroughly prepared and protected by wire entanglements. They attacked but failed to capture it.

6. A counter-attack was at once delivered before the Germans had time to make good their position, with the result that the enemy was driven out of the village again, leaving about 100 dead and 100 prisoners in our hands.

7. The lessons to be learned from this attack are :—

First, the need of good wire obstacles in front of the fire trenches. If a proper entanglement cannot be constructed on account of the proximity of the enemy's trenches, then *chevaux de frise* made of wooden supports with wire twisted across them can be pushed out in front of the parapet and anchored.

Secondly, the importance of providing a strongly constructed keep or reduit as a supporting point and pivot of manœuvre in rear of the front line of trenches.

Thirdly, the imperative necessity of launching a counter-attack at the earliest possible moment after the front line has been broken and before the enemy has been able to throw up any kind of improvised defences.

Attack on C

8. The attack was delivered in daylight, at 8.30 a.m., after very heavy and sustained bombardment by artillery, and was immediately preceded by fire from a trench-mortar and by the throwing of bombs. The front trenches were speedily captured by the Germans notwithstanding that the defenders had half-an-hour's warning of the impending attack.

9. The Germans followed up their success, but on reaching the keep, some hundred yards in rear of the front line of defences, they failed to make further progress.

10. The defenders had no guns in close support so that artillery fire was not brought to bear on the attackers after their success, and the latter therefore proceeded at once to entrench themselves. No counter-attack was made for four hours after the assault. The keep held out, but when the counter-attack was made it failed to re-establish the line.

11. There were no bomb-proofs or shelters of any kind near the front trenches in which the defenders could take cover during the bombardment.

12. The lessons to be learned from this attack are :—

First, the immense importance of a counter-attack being delivered at the earliest possible moment after the line has been broken.

Secondly, the imperative need of close artillery support and of guns being brought to bear at once on the lost trenches and the intervening ground, directed by artillery officers in observation posts from which the ground can be well seen.

Thirdly, the value of a strong keep, well wired in all round.

Fourthly, the need of bomb-proofs in which the defenders can take shelter during the artillery bombardment.

Fifthly, the value of bombs and hand-grenades with which to reply to the enemy when they begin bomb throwing. A good supply should be kept in the support trenches, to be available for a counter-attack should the fire trench be captured by the enemy. The positions of these supplies must be known to all concerned.

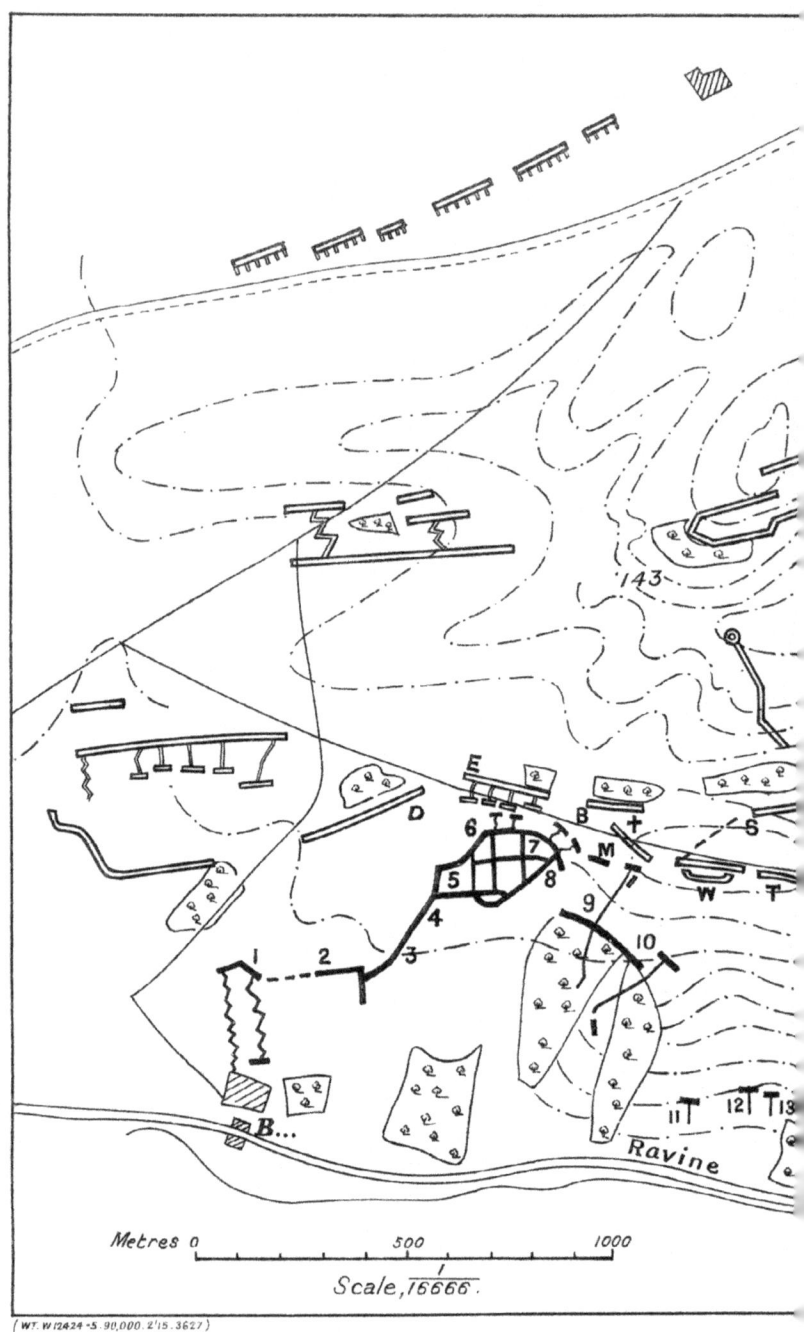

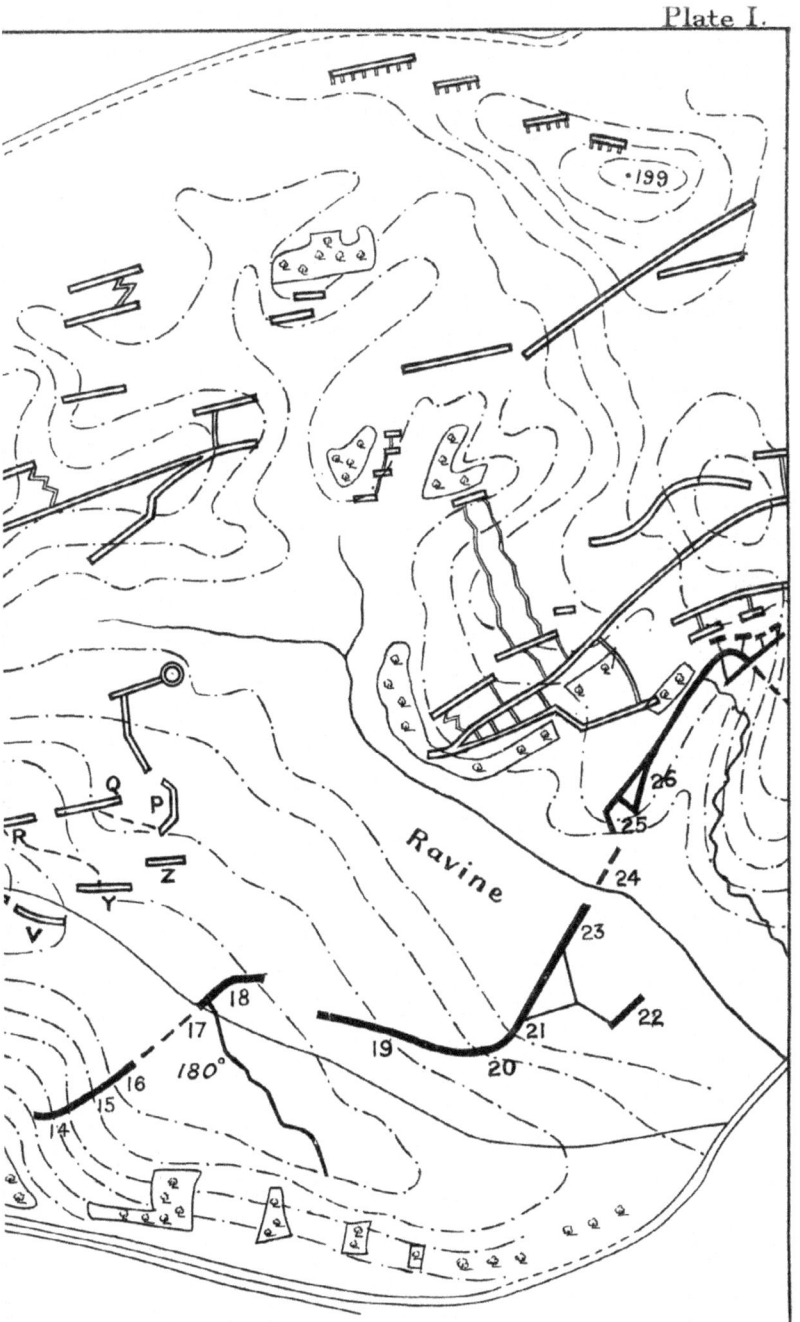

Plate I.

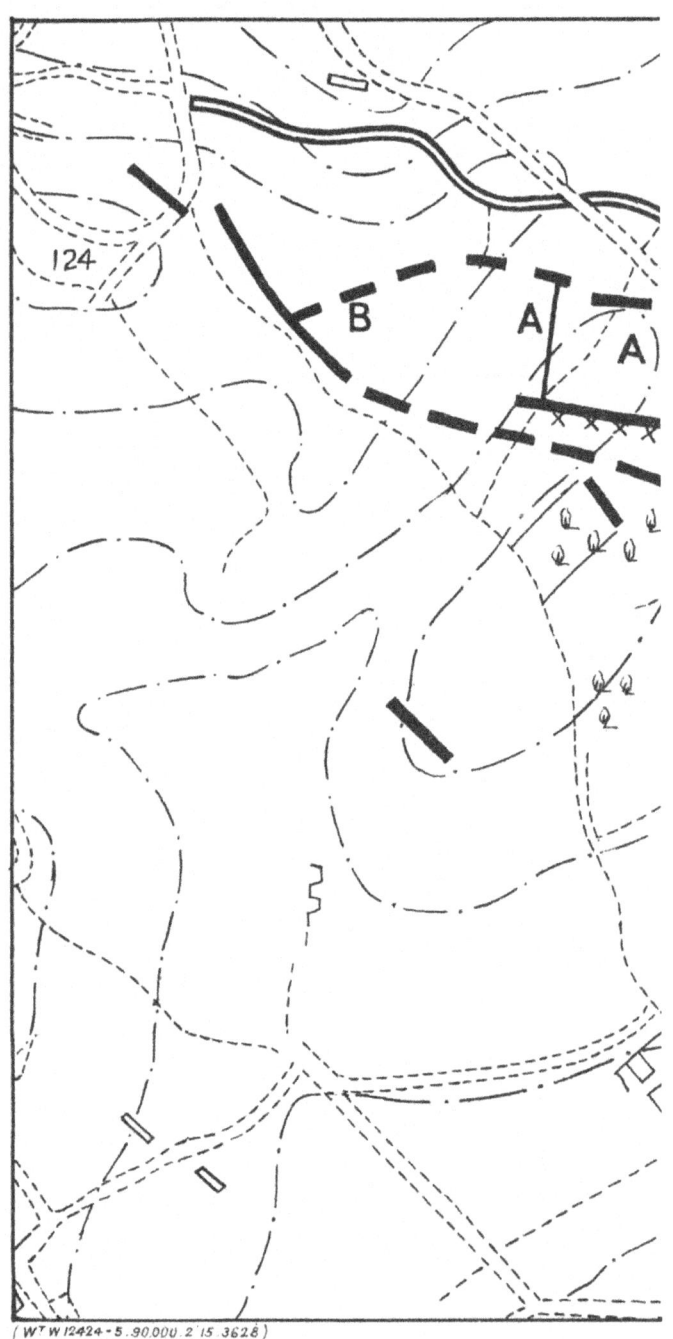

Plate II.

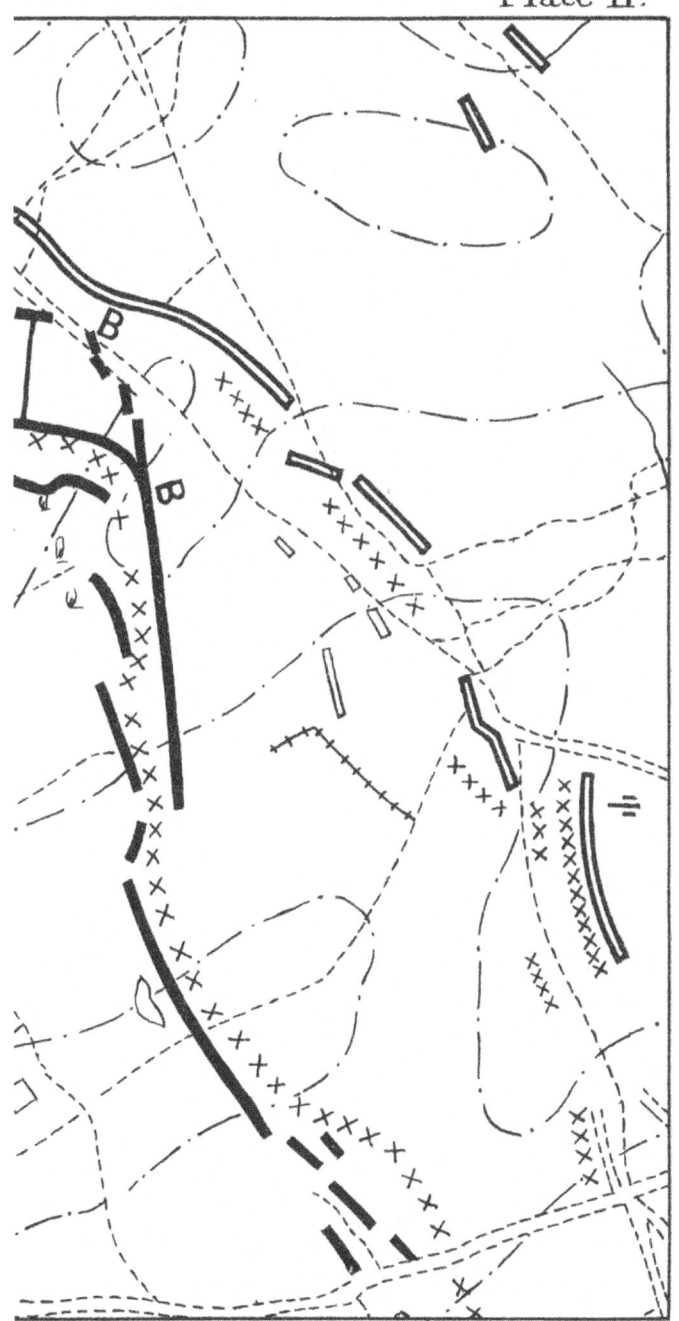

www.ingramcontent.com/pod-product-compliance
Lightning Source LLC
Chambersburg PA
CBHW040312050426
42450CB00020B/3469